Codependent No More

Life Can Be Better When You Overcome Codependency

By

MEGAN COULTER

Megan Coulter

"as is" without warranty or guarantee of any kind.

ACKNOWLEDGMENTS

For my students and friends, who all
selflessly helped me in writing this book?
Special thanks to those who asked, insisted
and assisted me in turning the seminars in
this practical form. All Rights Reserved
2012-2015 @ Megan Coulter

TABLE OF CONTENTS

Introduction

Chapter 1 - Understanding the World of Co-dependency

- To Help You Have Control over Your Life
- Stay Strong Even When Alone
- Move to the Top
- Respect Everyone around You

Chapter 2 - Knowing You Are Dependent

- I Cannot Do It without Him
- I Cannot Do It without Her
- I Need Them Here To Make This Happen
- They Must Help Me out At All Cost

Chapter 3 - Understanding the 5 W's Of Co-dependency

- **What**
- **Who**
- **Why**
- **When**
- **Where**

Chapter 4 - Process of Reaching a Life Free From Co-dependency

- **Immediate Process**
- **Quick Process**
- **Slow Process**

Chapter 5 - Counseling Others about Co-dependency

- **Children**
- **Youth**
- **Adult**
- **Elderly**

Chapter 6 - Having a Good Idea of Co-dependency Help

- **Practice Exactly What You Advise People to Do**
- **Make Your Views Clear To People You Know Are Co-dependent around You**

Chapter 7 - Healthy Dieting Helps To Build You Mentally

- **Eat Healthy Foods**
- **Try To Eat At Least 3 Times a Day**
- **Workout Regularly As Well**

Chapter 8 - The Bad Traits of Co-dependency

- **Insecurity**
- **Fear**
- **Manipulation**

Chapter 9 - Spot Co-dependency Traits in Your Children Early

Chapter 10 - Co-dependent Relationships

- Knowing You Are Dating a Co-dependent Partner
- How Do You Deal With a Co-dependent Partner?
- Trying To Control Your Co-dependent Partner

Chapter 11 - Use the Internet to Find out More about Co-dependent Behaviors

Chapter 12 - Try To Be Accommodating To Co-dependent People

- Be Nice To Them, But Do Not Allow Them Take You For Granted
- Try Your Best to Ignore the Things They Do

- **If Their Behavior Affects You Negatively, Get Rid Of Them**

Chapter 13 - Get the Help You Need

Chapter 14 - Read More about Co-dependency

FAQ

Disclaimer

INTRODUCTION

Have you ever come across or continuously heard the word 'codependency?' Well, if you have heard someone tell you or another person "you are codependent" then this eBook is meant for you. You should not only read more about codependency, you should also get to understand many aspects of it that affects us both negatively and positively. Although, most people do not actually or truly understand the word codependency, it has been branded to be a bad word. So, people who are told or referred to with this word do not have a good feeling about it.

This term has steadily developed quite a negative connotation that literally means someone who is clingy, needy and sick. Not all three literary meanings are words people will like to be referred to as. This is why reading this book will make you understand the word more and give you a whole new way of viewing it and also how to treat people whom you have realized have codependency issues.

You do not need to be told you are codependent in most instances especially those who are able to realize their misdoings earlier on. However, some people need reality checks in order to be able to know for real what is going on with them. Mostly, codependency is linked to or related to intimate relationships more. However, they have some small effects on the lives of people outside their intimate relationships.

CHAPTER 1

UNDERSTANDING THE WORLD OF CODEPENDENCY

Understanding the word codependence is the best tool to help you say to yourself '**Codependent No More**'. It is easy to say you are really ending this codependent lifestyle; however for so many people going through with this prevention is always the problem. So can codependency be considered as a pathological condition or just society or the world diagnosing some people wrongly and making them seem abnormal in a certain way?

Well, to be codependent is to be so highly dependent on something that you feel that thing is the only source of your happiness, living, wealth, affluence, peace, health, etc. So, if someone is considered or seen as codependent, it

13

means that he or she is not capable of taking important decisions on their own or making the best out of their lives without the help of another person – which is an ideal thing.

One of the greatest and deadly diseases in our world today is loneliness. Some people feel that they can gain anything they want or need when they become independent and get to the top. So, they let go of all ideas of codependence in their system chasing independence, and this leads them to a life of sadness.

Codependence is not a bad thing; it is mostly how people have stigmatized it and also how other people go about their codependency that causes problems.

To Help You Have Control Over Your Life

In our world today, the only people who are spared and understood to be codependent are children and growing adolescents or teenagers. Even with that, they are supposed to be codependent to their parents and not to anyone else. This should show you how weird our world is gradually becoming.

Some years ago, people loved to depend on and loved to help more than to be helped. However, it is not the same today. This is why for your very own good, there will be the need to help control your life or have some control over your life to prevent you having to be co-dependent on someone for happiness, money, peace, etc. Although being too dependent isn't good all the time, it is better than being overly co-dependent.

Stay Strong Even When Alone

Understanding the world of codependence and seeing how codependent people are painted black or made to look like they are worthless should be motivation enough for you to try your best to stay out of that circle. In the society in which we find ourselves in, the main values we move and live around are independence, achievement, and strength. This is why codependent people are not given a welcoming space at all.

Today, most men admire women who are independent, strong and self-sufficient. Yes, most men love to have women who do not need anyone to be complete, or so everyone thinks.

Although this is fair, a lot of independent people have also been codependent before. Yes, some people because of the realization of their codependent behavior or attitude moved to become independent or dependent.

All you need is to understand that the world doesn't want people who are needy and codependent. This is why it is a must for you to build your inner strength as well as make the most out of your life to be able to stand alone and not always need someone or anyone to give you happiness or to complete you.

Move To The Top

In moving to the top, you do not need to be codependent, and this is completely true. Being codependent at work is one thing that can make you lose respect before all your colleagues even when you are given a promotion. Being independent and making sure, you do not always need people to make specific decisions for you at your workplace shows a lot of maturities. It is this type of maturity that makes you stand out and gain respect.

The problem, however, is that a lot of people confuse independence to the level of selfish self-absorption or even worse as the determinant of a relationship's well-being. This is however, what has led to the high rates of loneliness in the world today with so many divorces, which have also increased the number of depression and suicidal cases all over the world.

Moving to the top is amazing and being independent is even better. However, try to have some little traces of codependency in your system because a little of it doesn't hurt and that is the truth.

Respect Everyone Around You

In your aim to reduce codependency in your life or to be codependent no more, you need to be very cautious. Some people feel that some of the good character traits they had when they were called or referred to as codependent must go away for them to be independent.

Well, this is a lie. So, if you were used to respecting and paying due honor to anyone or everyone around you do not need to change from that because you want to become independent or are reducing your level of codependency.

When you become independent and tend not to respect others around you, it affects you. This is because no one will like to be close to an independent person who doesn't respect others. Respect is one of the main bases the world moves on.

So, you will end up being a lonely independent man or woman because no one will be interested in getting closer to you. Loneliness is one of the main diseases that are killing us in today's age, and egoistic independence is one of the reasons for this.

CHAPTER 2
KNOWING YOU ARE DEPENDENT

To be codependent is far better than to be dependent. However, the problem with our world today is that most people are unable to differentiate between the both. To be codependent means to be needy in specific aspects of your life. For instance, some people are codependent when it comes to their relationships, their work, health, life, etc. To be dependent has to do with being completely needy and reliant on people in all aspects of your life.

However, dependency in a unique way is needed if we want to establish or build any type of relationship because we need to rely on others and also let them rely on us in a relationship. There is, however, a limit to every kind of dependability. To connect with another person's needs, sharing and also permitting you to be affected and influenced by that individual. Since the connection is needed to make a

19

relationship work, and it literally needs dependency to make that happen, even being a little dependent is not a bad thing after all. However, this doesn't dispute the fact that too much of everything is bad.

I Cannot Do It Without Him

This is one of the major mistakes that make dependency seem like a bad thing in all aspects of life. For instance, some people can be so dependent on their husbands or boyfriends or even their fathers that, they feel they cannot make important decisions without them. So ask yourself, 'what happens when they are not around or cannot be reached?'

If your mum needs surgery, and your father is not around, but the surgical procedure has been explained to you and needs to be done in few hours, what will you do? Some daughters are so dependent on their fathers that they cannot even approve of a man to be their husband if their father doesn't approve.

Also, most of them will break up with the man they consider the love of their lives just because their daddy said

20

they should. This is bad. Yes, this kind of dependency ruins the world and is one of the reasons why there is so much pain in the hearts of people and high levels of loneliness and depression.

Just make sure you grow with the mindset that you can do anything and make any decision without the most important people of your life being around. There are times that you still need to take specific decisions on your own even when they are around. Your life is your life, and that is it.

I Cannot Do It Without Her

I cannot do it without her; this is a phrase a lot of men who are attached to their moms say. It is funny how grown men and even some women can be so attached or dependent on their mother's or some relationships that they fail to see the realities of life. The truth about life is that, no matter how much you try as a man, your mother will be gone someday. This is why you will hear so many people complain about how they would wish to have their mothers around to make specific or certain decisions in their lives for them. Yes, such people were very dependent on their mother's, and this affects them in their daily lives as they grow especially when they lose them.

I Need Them Here To Make This Happen

This phrase is mostly heard when people are involved in some kind or sort of competition or want to do some kind of business deal together in a group. You need to understand that you will not always find members of your family or people in a group to be as attached to your vision and dreams as you are.

This is why you always need to be somewhat independent and always prepared to make the right presentations to make sure all deals and competitions are won even without their support. Having the moral support of the people, you love matters a lot, but it is not everything.

This doesn't mean however that, if they turn out to be disappointing or are unable to make it or come to your aid like you wanted, you should end everything and throw a business deal that was yours to handle or competition you could have won away.

You will go on in life blaming them for causing pain to you. However, you are the only to blame for such decisions because you made those decisions at that time. Being dependent and codependent is amazing; however, you should never make it cloud your sense of good judgment.

They Must Help Me Out At All Cost

A lot of depending and codependent people live their lives with the notion that everyone owes them a favor. This is a big issue that people have thrown so many years of their lives away thinking. The first rule of life, you need to know whether you are dependent or codependent is that you owe no one anything, and no one owes you anything. Yes. If you decide to love someone, you do not owe it to the person to love you back.

The person you love is the one who decides to love you back. If you give someone some money for free, you do not owe it to them to give you back the money. They are the only ones who can decide if they want to give you back the money or return a favor when you are in great need for similar help.

So you see, never say someone or some people need to help you at all costs because help is not something you can force. It is either they want to help you or they do not want to help you, end of story. Instead of trying to ask people for everything and doing nothing to warrant the help you ask for, try to be independent and take control of most aspects of your life.

It might not be easy, and codependency, as well as dependency, will come in from time to time. However, make independence and strength your main tools for life and you will see a better way forward.

CHAPTER 3

UNDERSTANDING THE 5 W'S OF CODEPENDENCE

WHAT

What is codependence? The word codependence has to do with an attitude or character trait that is adapted or natural to some people. This character trait has to do with people always depending somehow on people to make their lives whole.

Although a lot of people have helped to make this word quite unpleasant to hear, a lot of things come together to determine if codependency in a particular person is bad or good. Also, codependency is never bad entirely. It mostly has to do with who is considered as codependent and how they go about the process.

WHO

Who can be considered co-dependent? Every human being in some unique way is codependent on another person. For instance, you work in a law firm, and you have a boss. So, even if you are the most independent lawyer in the world, you still need your boss to pay you salary. This means you are co-dependent on him for this reason. Also, storeowners need or are codependent on their clients or customers to come and shop for them so that they can make more money.

These few examples in the text above show that codependence is seen everywhere in our day-to-day lives. This means that anyone and everyone can be considered as codependent. However, the level of co-dependence is what can be quite a cause for worry.

WHY

So, why is codependency seen to be so bad? This is the problem a lot of people especially psychologists are finding it hard to believe. No one knows where the notion of codependency being a bad thing or bad word came to the place. However, it has for some reason become a forbidden word that a lot of people do not want to hear or even want to be referred to as. Well, codependency is not a bad character trait to have at all if you know some of the benefits it brings.

Some people have had a bad intimate relationship as well as cordial relationship issues with people with bad codependent attitudes. This, however, doesn't mean that to be codependent is the worst thing on earth or even very bad. Also, codependency some years ago was linked more too intimate relationships; however, these relationships can be seen in offices, homes, schools, etc.

WHEN

When do I realize codependency in another person? A lot of people are never seen as codependent till they show a specific character trait. This is why you should never feel you are completely or totally in control of your life. There are times when our emotions and thoughts take over our actions. This is why you should never judge people wrongly and try to seem all perfect where codependency issues are concerned. Below are some signs of codependency you need to know of:

- **Impaired boundaries**
- **Find it difficult to maintain their sense of self in relationships**
- **Feel they are rejected when important people in their lives spend time with other friends without them**
- **Always, want their partners to show them the same or more love in relationships**
- **Highly sensitive to rejections**
- **Their relationships are idealized**
- **Has high tendency towards depression**

These signs above and more are not so bad. However, they can get worse depending on the setting of what is going on and the kind of person being considered or seen as codependent as well as how you treat the individual. When you realize that your friend, family member, colleague or partner has codependency issues, you need to help them control the trait and not try to make them feel or look infervor.

WHERE

Where do I get help for my codependency issues? If you have realized that you are codependent, then you might have gone too far with this character to have sacked or pushed people you love and care about away. Getting help for extreme codependency at work or in your intimate or personal relationships should not be something to be shy about. It is better to realize you have a problem and make sure it is fixed than to live your life in complete isolation and loneliness not knowing why people like you today and push you out tomorrow.

If you cannot read books and other resources online to build the independence and strength you need, you can visit a psychologist to help you out. These health experts have the highest level of understanding in codependency, and they can guide you to become a better independent and strong you. One of the reasons why people are not advised to go for codependent transformation on their own is the way they go about the process.

A lot of people have transformed from codependent nice and lovely people to independent cold and uncaring people. This is why going to an expert for the right help matters. Most codependents go too far when they try to recover from their former traits, and this doesn't help.

This happens because as they mostly become independent and start to regret how codependent they were that they try too hard to fix those errors from the past, which do not matter anymore. So, to be on the safer side, try to be calm and still keep the good traits in there. Do not feel being independent means treating people less understanding of who you are and making them feel weak.

If you didn't like the way you were treated because people claimed you were too codependent, then try to help others get out of it too.

CHAPTER 4

PROCESS OF REACHING A LIFE FREE FROM CODEPENDENCY

The processes of life in all aspects, when realized, helps to make us better and gives us a clear sense of what we need to put in place as well as that what we need to make our priority. Reaching the life that is free from codependency is not completely possible because no matter what, you need to co depend on people as you move on to life.

Codependence can be very normal; however, you always need to try not to abuse overly its use because that is what generates problems for you. Below are some of the processes you can take to reaching a life that is free from codependency. The level at which you decide to go will solely depend on you. However, try your very best to make the right decisions and do right no matter what.

Immediate Process

There is the immediate process of when people get rejected or get called codependent once and decide to relax, check their lives and work towards building their strengths and independence. When this happens, such people are able to check their lives and make sure they find the right resources and help to help them stay free and clean from high codependency traits.

This immediate process helps to take you out from the dark as soon as possible and makes you stronger and better. However, you are completely in charge of where you obtain the necessary information you need to transform which helps. Every human being has the ability to become independent even as they maintain a level of attachment to their loved ones. If you are able to achieve this by the immediate process, then it is best.

Quick Process

There is also the quick process of realization and getting rid of. Although the quick process has to do more with finding your ground the quick way, it takes a longer way than the immediate process. This way has more to do with an individual making sure the process that they go through is done with full commitment and assurance that they really want to leave the world of complete codependence on others.

The tendency of people is going the wrong way or getting rid of the good attitudes they have low with this process. So, try your very best to get through with this way for your very own good. Although codependence is not a bad thing, there is the need for you to know how your codependence on people and things can be controlled so that you do not suffer for it.

Slow Process

The funny thing about the slow process of freeing yourself from high codependence is the fact that, only a few people are able to control their codependence in the shorter period. This happens because all through this process they can be faced with both good and bad decisions to make and if the tendency of an individual to make bad decisions is higher than the good ones, then there is a problem. The slow process however if handled very well can yield higher results than all other processes.

All processes, however, need acknowledging and confronting in order for them to be changed. So, keep it in mind that the process to change is in itself a process, but not an event. When you confront your reality and accept that you are doing something wrong without feeling bad or feeling that everyone hates you, you will then need to decide the right steps for you or the right processes to fix your problems.

Also, with perseverance and the needed effort, you can definitely change these habits and make the most out of your life.

CHAPTER 5

COUNSELING OTHERS ABOUT CODEPENDENCY

If you grew up in a life where you did everything you were asked or told to do, like a good girl or boy, there are some codependent foundations that are built in your life. There are so many good things that come with codependency that we should celebrate. However, this doesn't mean that you should not counsel others about codependency issues when you know you can and find yourself in a better state or level.

A lot of people fail to understand that their lives revolve around codependency on others. However, if the level of codependency is above 75%, then there is a problem.

CHILDREN

Codependent children can be counseled, but it should be done in a unique way to make sure they do not feel you hate them. Naturally, children are codependent, and this is because they should be. From the age of infancy, they need their parents to feed them, bathe them, clothe them, wash their clothes, help them walk and for so many other things. However, as they grow into kindergarten age, their true selfstarts to be shown. This is where you get to know if there is the need to correct them or not.

If your child moves from codependency in the home and starts to be too codependent on friends at school and the neighborhood then, you need to be careful. Make sure you advise your child in a pleasant way that they can be independent in a unique way. There are so many children movies as well as storybooks and cartoons you can benefit from in giving them this counseling.

So, buy the best ones and with them, you will just have to enjoy the movie with them and try to base on the movie to advise them, which takes their mind off the real reason why you are telling them what you are saying.

YOUTH

There is nothing wrong about youth being codependent. However, their codependence should be checked. Most teenage girls and boys during their teenage periods tend to take a certain level of co-dependence that harms them a lot. Some teenage boys join the bad company at school because they want to fit in and need those friends at school to feel better about themselves. This applies to some girls especially in cheerleading clubs.

If you want to counsel a teenager about codependency, make sure you start with stories. Telling them a story about your past and getting them interested will help you to give them a solution to their codependency problems. This will help to build a better life and also bring you together more. So that, they can share their problems with you every time they need someone to talk to.

Codependent teenagers are loyal and make the best of friends. However, they can be taken for granted and this is why you need to guide your teenage daughter or son on the right path. If you do not, they might end up being taken advantage of and left aside which will build pain and hurt in their hearts.

ADULT

Who else can be there for you in the middle of the night when you need them? Well, codependent friends are simply amazing. Due to the fact that they expect you to show them love in the same way and appreciate them in the same way too, they will do anything and everything to make you happy.

For individuals or adults who know what highly independent people bring to the table, they love to make friends with codependent people. However, there are times when the codependency of some people is too high which is why you need to be very careful how you go about trying to correct or help your codependent friends.

Most times, when you try to tell your codependent friends about their codependent attitudes being bad, they end up feeling you do not like them anymore or something such, which should not be so. Make sure your codependent friends are closer to you when you realize their weakness. This will make it easier to help them than when they are far from you. Also, never make them feel like they are stupid because that will only worsen matters and make them start to hate.

ELDERLY

The elderly, when they get to a certain age, become very codependent on their children for their very basic needs. The elderly can be quite annoying when they get to this stage especially after their retirement when they have nothing to do or nowhere to go. They mostly feel their children and grandchildren should leave their important duties and other jobs just to sit around and talk with them.

This codependent levels if not followed through like it should make them lonely and increase their chances of becoming suicidal or depressed which is not good. You can try to get these codependency attitudes from your elderly guardian or friend by trying to be there when you can.

CHAPTER 6

HAVING A GOOD IDEA OF CODEPENDENCY HELP

Try to read more about codependency because it helps you to understand codependent people better and also helps you know how to treat codependent people. To know more about this unique character trait, make sure you read more and more about the different codependency levels available. There are books and websites available that you get to benefit from where such information and details are concerned.

The more you know about codependency, the better for you. Codependent people make the best of friends and employees. These are some of the good traits they have come with naturally.

Practice Exactly What You Advise People To Do

If you are a codependent person, there is the need for you to know how to benefit from this character trait and nothing else. Codependent people are generally creative and try all the time to find new solutions to problems to make others happy because most of them base their happiness on the happiness of others. Codependent people are givers, and they always want to be treated fairly. As a codependent person make sure you preach what you teach other codependent people below:

- **It is far better to give others than to receive**
- **Codependents do not receive compliments very well**
- **They love their neighbors even when not invited into their problems**
- **They are naturally reliant partially on people.**

If you have been able to deal with your codependency issues, try to help others to do the same in order for them to understand better their lives.

Make Your Views Clear To People You Know Are Codependent Around You

Although codependent people can be lovely to have around, there are some codependent people that go to the extreme. If you have this kind of extreme codependent friends around you, then there will be the need to make them know in a nice way that their character is affecting you.

Try to be very clear with them and share your views openly and calmly so that you do not have to hurt their feelings when you go about telling them. When you tell them in a nice way, it makes it easier for them to get the help they need from you.

CHAPTER 7

HEALTHY DIETING HELPS TO BUILD YOU MENTALLY

One of the ways you can help to build the mentality or mental strength of a codependent person is through healthy dieting. Although a lot of people do not take this seriously, healthy dieting helps a lot to build the mental strength of co-dependent people. This helps to make it easy for them to learn how to balance codependency and independent traits together.

Eat Healthy Foods

Eating healthy foods has to do with eating balanced diets and eating the very best of vegetables, fruits, etc. Also, making sure, you eat healthy and natural, non-chemical foods will help you as well.

Eating brown sugar, brown rice, brown bread, lean meat, cabbages, spinaches, carrots, oranges, bananas, tangerines, apples, berries, grapes, and others helps a lot.

Try To Eat At Least 3 Times A Day

Try you're very best to eat at least 3 times each and every day. Try to spread your meals across the day and also make sure you eat fruits and more vegetables during the day. This will help to keep your brain active all the time and sharp as well.

Workout Regularly As Well

Regular exercises or workouts help a lot as well. You get to relax and get rid of unwanted toxins. So, make sure you take that also very seriously for your health especially.

CHAPTER 8

THE BAD TRAITS OF CODEPENDENCE

There are so many good reasons why codependent people should not be taken for granted in our society because they form the strong basis for our communities. However, the truth about how bad their situation can be especially when they have higher levels of some bad traits should not be taken for granted or forgotten. Below are some of the bad traits of codependency you need to be aware of:

INSECURITY

Codependent people can be highly insecure. Yes, they lack self-esteem in so many instances and cases, which does a lot to affect them. They find it very difficult to meet their very own needs and wants as well as their inability to understand and know who they actually are. Their high sense of insecurity can make them feel very sensitive to rejection along with high levels of jealous, possessive and emotions.

Insecurity is very normal to every human being; however being overly insecure to the extent that you get to damage, almost anything good that comes your way can be quite dangerous. So, the level of insecurity in these people depending on their level of codependency can be very high or low.

FEAR

Every human being has some kind of fear in them. What might make some people very scared might not make others scared. This is why you need to understand it when people are frightened. However, where codependent people are concerned, the level of fear can be amazingly out of this world.

Yes, highly codependent people can have great fear, not of the darkness alone like most of us reasonably do. They mostly fear they will be heartbroken in relationships, fear if they do not receive a call from their partners, always feel that people are plotting against them in the workplace if they are not added or included in a discussion, fear they might die tomorrow, fear if they do not please their friends they will leave them alone, etc.

Not all of these thoughts are helpful. They bring you down as a person and never make you feel better about yourself in any way. This is one character trait that can be taken to the extreme where codependent people are concerned, and this should be checked.

MANIPULATION

Codependent people love to manipulate people to feeling pity for them all the time, and they do this to make sure they win some favors or get people to stay with them continually. Although manipulation might not be so bad, there are so many reasons why it should not be welcomed in the world of today.

Manipulative skills, when enhanced, can cause or bring a lot of problems to you especially if you have a codependent manipulative person as your friend. So, if you have tried for so many years, but still cannot get your friend to free him or herself from the manipulative codependency issues they have, which affect you, try to distance yourself from them for your own good.

CHAPTER 9

SPOT CODEPENDENCY TRAITS IN YOUR CHILDREN EARLY

Spotting codependency traits in your children at the early stages of their life can help save them from a life of rejection and uncertainty in the future. Below are some tips to show you your children are hitting the codependency road:

- **They try to not do things on their own without your help**
- **Fight with their siblings to gain attention**
- **Stay away from you when you have the children of others**
- **Bear grudges easily and love to stay away**
- **Do well for a benefit or reward**

CHAPTER 10

CODEPENDENT RELATIONSHIPS

Most times, there are so many people who worry about their relationships because they are with codependent partners or spouses. Most times, the partner who shows codependent traits may try to safeguard his or her own emotions by trying to avoid the love given.

Codependent partners can go to a greater level or extent just to have their love reciprocated by their partners, and when this doesn't happen, it kills them. If you have a feeling that you are not in a healthy relationship, make sure you first and foremost check the relationship out for any obsessive attitudes or tendencies.

This will help you understand the whole world of codependency in relationships and how you can deal or manage to live with your codependent partner happily.

Knowing You Are Dating A Codependent Partner

A lot of people stay with codependent partners for so many years tolerating their bad codependency tendencies without knowing they are dating a codependent person. Your very own feelings are very important in appraising the relationship you are in. You can find out that your partner is a codependent person, but still try your best to stay and make things work out.

A common way to know you are dating a codependent partner is that they mostly feel insecure and feel they are not good enough all the time. Although they love you, they might act in fear all the time because of some issues they maybe had to face as children and the emotional experiences they have carried along with them to adulthood from childhood.

If the problems you have are with your partner having to do with or revolve around codependency of one partner, you can come together and try to deal with it as a team. This is the most effective way of solving this problem. You are the only person who can tell if the relationship you are in is healthy or not. So, with those who do not even have obsessive tendencies, you can definitely have codependent faces of their relationships.

The difference, however, is the level of codependency in relationships and if partners are willing to learn how to adapt to one another without having to sacrifice their very own emotional necessities.

How Do You Deal With A Codependent Partner?

Dealing with codependent partners can be quite difficult especially if you do not know what to do or how to go about the process. Codependent partners should be dealt with care. If you find out your partner is codependent, you need to try your best to relax and try to be more caring and loving. However, this should be done in a way that your codependent partner doesn't feel they are getting your way.

Try your best to talk to them and advise them on how they can deal with the process. The reason why you cannot blame codependent partners so much is the fact that, most of these people have reached the level of codependency that they have reached because of past and childhood experiences.

If you, however, feel like you cannot or are not ready to deal with the problem, try your best to seek the expert help of a psychologist to help. Psychologists and counselors have a way of making sure your partner has the right help and support.

Trying To Control Your Codependent Partner

No matter how much you realize that you love your codependent partner, there is the need to be in control of the relationship and make sure you are not been manipulated. People with extreme codependency issues tend to be very demanding and also manipulative. This is why you need to be very careful in order to deal with them. To control codependent partners, you need to understand what is really going on. Also, you need to put the fact that you love them too much to hurt them aside.

Maybe someone has told you some time ago that your partner is self-destructive due to some previous relationships he or she has been in or you have evaluated your partner and have realized that they have codependency issues, make sure you find a way to make them desist from the extremeness of this tendency.

It is very normal for codependent people to be stuck or to find themselves in many unhealthy relationships because of their belief that they do not deserve love and that every single person who loves them today will go away eventually. Below are some points to consider in controlling or managing your codependent partner in a relationship or even at the workplace:

- Cut the codependent person off in a nice way and try not to entertain him or her so much like you used to do in the past.

- Encourage the codependent partner or person to find something they love to do on their own or a hobby. This will help them to believe they can be happy and enjoy stuff on their own. Help them from a distance to become better when you see they are going wrong in specific parts and truly need your help.

If you truly love and care for your codependent partner, it can be hell to manage such relationships. However, it is not a problem if you make the effort to help them.

CHAPTER 11

USE THE INTERNET TO FIND OUT MORE ABOUT CODEPENDENT BEHAVIORS

The internet is the hub of information today. This is why you should never take the information you obtain online about codependent behaviors and everything about it for granted. If you want to use the internet to research and know more about codependency tendencies, read the points below:

- Online research always helps. Make sure you do not stick to cheap sites that do not have credible content to offer you.
- Speak to psychologists for help. There are psychologists online who will be willing to help you without taking any money. So, you can contact them as well.

- Do not go about thinking everyone around you is codependent.

CHAPTER 12

TRY TO BE ACCOMMODATING TO CODEPENDENT PEOPLE

Accommodating and accepting codependent people for who they are and understanding how you can live with them helps them become better people. So, try to be nice and do not see them be needy. Read the following points to know some of the things to do where they are concerned:

- **Be nice to them, but do not allow them take you for granted**

- **Try your best to ignore the things they do**

- **If their behavior affects you negatively, get rid of them**

CHAPTER 13

GET THE HELP YOU NEED

It can be difficult for a codependent person to accept the problem he or she has and decide to get the right help needed. However, when this happens, it is good news that needs to be celebrated. The fact that you are codependent and have been rejected by people who do not understand how unique you are should be the motivation for you to get help. Below are some steps you need to take to your freedom and happiness especially where extreme codependency issues are concerned:

- **Realize you have a problem**

- **Go to an expert for help**

Be ready to build your relationship

CHAPTER 14

READ MORE ABOUT CODEPENDENCY

Reading is very important. To understand the different worlds of codependency, there is the need for you to find ways to read more about this character trait. There is so much that you need to know about codependency to appreciate people with this character trait as well as how to deal with them. If reading this eBook is not enough for you and you want to read more books that are specific to the different ways codependency affects likes positively and negatively, the internet is the best place to obtain all the information you need.

The human system is a very complicated configuration that you can navigate or operate. Although this eBook is detailed, it doesn't specify specific aspects of life. Dry addicts have a higher tendency of having codependency personalities or issues. The only problem of codependent people is that they tend not to function very well on their own. They rather organize their thoughts and attitudes about substances, persons, and processes.

Check The Internet To Buy Books

Today, the internet is filled with so many different books and articles on codependency and all it covers. You are the one who needs to take buying and reading these books very seriously. The more you buy and read these books, the better you experience the true beauty of co-dependent people.

Buying books on the internet will open your eyes to a whole new world of codependency understanding. There are books that deal directly with codependency in relationships. With these books, you will get to understand that in codependent relationships, obsessive traits can ruin the health of a relationship and also ruin the partnership the relationship has.

FAQ

- **Is it so bad to be codependent on my boyfriend?**

There is nothing wrong if you are codependent on your boyfriend. You, however, need to be very cautious how you go about showing your codependency on your boyfriend. However, going to the extreme can lead to so many problems for you and might end your relationship. So, just try your best to blend your independence and codependency traits together for your own good.

- **How can I find codependency traits on a first date?**

There are so many ways you can find codependency traits in an individual on a first date with them. However, the most effective way to find these traits is by ensuring you ask your date a lot of questions about their lives and their views on life in general. Delving deep into the lives of these people will help you know them more. Finding codependency traits in your date should not push you away from them; it should make you want to know them better and want to be around them more. Remember, codependency is never a bad thing.

- **Can I try to live with a codependent partner?**

Yes. You can try and succeed loving and living with a codependent person. However, this will only happen when you read more about codependency and understand it.

- **Can codependency affect my sense of reasoning?**

Codependency depending on its levels can affect your sense of reasoning negatively or positively. However, you control how much it affects you in every way.

- **Should I be worried if my child shows codependency traits?**

Depending on how you are able to spot out these traits and deal with it, there is mostly nothing to be worried about. Your child can easily be straightened and freed from codependency traits especially if they are getting extreme.

- **I feel my colleagues are co-dependent on me. What do I do?**

If your colleagues are too co-dependent on you and it affects you and stresses you out, then make sure they know. Do not allow it to happen for long because the longer it happens, the more they expect from you, which can be very annoying. Try to tell them in a nice way for your own good and for peace to reign.

DISCLAIMER

This eBook has been written to give all readers an insight on how to reduce their codependence attitudes and also blend them together with other traits to give you a better life. All pages in this book are original, and there is no content copied from anywhere in this eBook from any website or book. This means the owner of this eBook needs to be contacted if all or any contents in the eBook are required to be made use of other sites and eBooks or books.

The different materials that are written or made available in this eBook are sole or unique to this site alone. Also, the website makes no warranties, and also disregards and takes for granted all other warranties, in addition to without self-control, indirect warranty, or some other breach of rights.

In addition, the website does not call for or make any images concerning the accuracy, feasible results, or reliability of the use of the materials on this website or if not linking to such materials or on any websites related to this website.

Printed in the USA
CPSIA information can be obtained
at www.ICGtesting.com
CBHW021005240924
14844CB00013B/68